Missing links
Settling national transport priorities

A CBI discussion document

© Published by the Confederation of British Industry,
Centre Point, 103 New Oxford Street, London WC1A 1DU

CBI members price £7.50
Non-members price £15
ISBN 0 85201 479 1
January 1995

Printed by Gwynprint, Hurstpierpoint, Sussex.
Typesetting Inner Vision Ltd, London EC1

Cover illustration: Jeorge Asare-Djan

Contents

Foreword

Introducing the report by the Standing Advisory Committee on Trunk Road Assessment (SACTRA) last December, Brian Mawhinney, Secretary of State for Transport, called for an active national debate on transport policy. Commenting on the report, The Financial Times noted that 'Transport policy is in a parlous state'.

The CBI reached that view a year ago. We could see that the forward programme set out in our 1989 report 'Trade Routes to the Future', which had been largely endorsed by the Government up to then, was unlikely to be completed. Government funding, which had been expanded at the end of the 1980s, had once again been sharply cut back and environmental opposition to new road schemes, whether widening or greenfield, was growing. As a result, many in the business community had entirely lost confidence in the direction of transport policy.

We were also aware, from our close links with the business communities in other European countries, that the same tensions can be found in France, Germany and elsewhere. The tension between the need for a transport infrastructure to support competitive business and resistance to the inevitable environmental disruption which the construction of such an infrastructure brings is common to all industrial countries.

But it seemed to us that these tensions are more constructively resolved elsewhere than they are in the United Kingdom. We therefore decided to carry out an examination of the way in which transport policy is devised in France, Germany and The Netherlands, to see what lessons could be learned for the UK.

The essential point which emerges is the importance of consensus. Other European countries reach consensus on the long term shape of their transport policies, consensus which brings stability and consistency in execution and allows businesses to plan for the future. Businesses have greater confidence in long term infrastructure plans announced by Governments, because their experience is that those plans, once announced, are carried through.

We need to find a better way of reaching decisions on transport policy in the UK if we are to remain competitive. We therefore propose to move on from the publication of this report to help push forward the debate on national transport policy which the Secretary of State wishes to see. We shall involve environmental groups, and others with an important point of view, in that process.

Our aim is to create a climate in which a new consensus on transport policy can be reached, one which reconciles the demands of a competitive economy with the environmental concerns which matter to us all.

Howard Davies
Director-General

Executive summary

Changes made in recent years by businesses to improve competitiveness (eg use of Just-In-Time production methods) have placed greater emphasis on the need for high-quality, cost-effective and reliable transport links. Good international links are also important for access to European markets, and enhancing the UK's attraction, both as a base for inward investment and as a tourist destination.

Considerable improvements have taken place in the competitive delivery of transport services in the UK and by UK carriers abroad, consistent with the liberalising emphasis of Government transport policy since the 1980s.

The relatively positive signs about the operation of services in the UK do not reflect the quality of UK transport infrastructure. In general, our infrastructure is worse affected by capacity and age constraints than that serving our main competitors in Europe.

The differences between countries in terms of the state of transport links is supported by qualitative evidence from business users of transport. It is also explained, at least in part, by the UK's past under-investment in transport compared with other European countries.

The Government's range of policy options to reverse this situation is, in practice, becoming increasingly restricted as it tries to set transport policy which is environmentally sustainable and consistent with a general aim to control public spending. But Governments in the other study countries - while facing the same broad constraints - have in place major investment programmes to improve yet further their transport networks.

The decision by Governments in France, Germany and the Netherlands actively to improve their transport links reflects three key strengths in the processes by which transport policy priorities are set, compared with the UK:

- There is a more strategic approach to improving transport links. Transport is seen as part of wider policies to encourage economic development while seeking (to differing degrees) to accommodate future traffic growth in an environmentally sustainable manner

- There is broader political and public ownership of key strategic objectives. This results from more effort being put into building a consensus on policy and priorities

■ Governments are more willing to make political and financial long-term commitments to deliver agreed objectives.

However, there are also weaknesses in the way in which transport priorities are decided in the study countries:

■ Infrastructure plans have sometimes fallen behind schedule and Governments have, in some cases, failed to implement politically difficult measures

■ All four study countries are trying to reduce perceived delay in their planning processes

■ The drive to attract greater private investment in transport is less developed in the three continental countries compared with the UK.

This report proposes for discussion a number of possible improvements to the UK decision-making process:

■ The Government must set out what is desirable - economically, environmentally and socially - in terms of developing key transport corridors. This should be done in the form of a policy paper which draws together a national framework for land use, infrastructure and transport services

■ The policy paper should set out a vision lasting at least 20 years into the future, within which there should be a five year rolling programme, reviewed annually to determine the progress of policies in meeting objectives. The cost of implementing national transport priorities over that period should be included, taking into account possible private funding where appropriate

■ Consideration should be given to forming a Cabinet sub-committee on transport, bringing together the DoT, DoE, DTI and Treasury, to strengthen cross-departmental ownership of policy

■ There must be an opportunity for the policy paper to be debated in public, by introducing it first as a Green Paper

■ A consistent investment appraisal methodology must be used on main transport corridors to evaluate alternative schemes, even if they involve different modes, to improve public confidence in the process through which investment decisions are made

■ The policy paper must be supported by a clear statement of the mix of policy instruments (eg pricing and public investment) to achieve objectives if the private sector is to have greater confidence in investing in transport

■ Government should develop medium-term contracts with providers of transport services and infrastructure, setting out a commitment by Government to provide funding where necessary to achieve improvements which satisfy strategic objectives. There should be penalty clauses for avoidable failure to meet commitments on both sides; and consideration should be given to contractual arrangements whereby Government can share in the profits generated by particularly successful schemes

■ The growing provision of infrastructure and services by the private sector offers a challenge, but not necessarily a threat, to the development of multi-modal transport strategy. Consideration should be given to establishing an Intermodal Panel, bringing together public and private sectors, along the lines of the Private Finance Panel, to improve the links between different forms of transport

■ Economic indicators of how the transport network performs should be developed alongside safety and environmental indices to help measure the effectiveness of policies.

Chapter 1

Introduction

1 Effective transport networks are an essential part of a strong internationally competitive economy. Companies whose goods and employees are on the move want networks which can consistently deliver good journey times with minimum disruption to customer services. Business investors want to be sure that network improvement will keep pace with economic growth. And those providing and investing in transport services need certainty in the framework of public policy, if they are to make the long term commitments often required.

2 There is widespread discontent in the business community about the failure of Government transport policy to meet these needs. Congestion on the roads is damaging the reliability of journey times; recent changes to the railways have led to major uncertainty about the future shape, size and quality of the network; and further development of key airports has been questioned.

3 That discontent has been accentuated by the announcement in the 1994 Budget of further spending cuts for the Department of Transport. Businesses are concerned that environmental arguments, such as those advanced by the Royal Commission on Environmental Pollution, now dominate the debate on transport policy at the expense of concern about UK competitiveness.

4 The lack of a long-term strategic framework for transport policy is thought by many to lie at the heart of these problems and is seen as an important reason why the UK's transport infrastructure is worse than that on the Continent. This report sets out to test that view and to assess whether the Government could do a better job if a clearer vision for transport provision was in place.

5 In trying to answer these questions, we have looked at experience in three other European countries - which also suffer from similar constraints in terms of tight budgets and environmental pressures - to see how decisions about transport policy are made. Our research has drawn not just on material supplied by Governments and transport providers, but also the views of business users of infrastructure and services in those countries.

6 It should be noted that this report focuses very much on policy-making at the national level. That is not to say that policy at the European and local levels is not important. However, where relevant, references have been made to practice in these areas.

7 No one country can be said to have developed a perfect model, and businesses elsewhere in Europe are also critical of their Governments. But lessons for the UK can be usefully learned from the experiences of France, Germany and the Netherlands. This report focuses on those lessons.

8 But, first: how far is it true that, from a business viewpoint, UK transport links are less satisfactory than those elsewhere in Europe?

Chapter 2

The current quality of UK transport links

9 In recent years, businesses have been changing the way in which they operate in order to become more competitive through, for example:

- Growing pan-European and global organisation of businesses

- Contracting-out of non-core functions (for example, support services like maintenance of office equipment)

- Use of leaner production methods (such as Just-In-Time in the retail and manufacturing sectors).

10 These developments mean that a transport network which consistently delivers reliable and quick journey times, at a competitive price, has become increasingly important to the efficient running of business. That applies not just to the major transport corridors serving inter-business trade, but also to the local transport networks which enable individuals to get to work and to retail and leisure facilities efficiently and without fuss.

11 For British firms, there is an added dimension. The UK's location on the edge of the European single market - the destination for over half of the UK's exports - emphasises the need for good links to the Continent. Our continuing success as a base for inward investment, as a distribution hub for North America and the Far East and as a tourist destination, also rely heavily on the effectiveness of our international communications.

The operation of transport services

12 In recent years, considerable improvements have taken place in the competitive delivery of transport services in the UK and by UK carriers abroad. The results have been impressive:

- The UK civil aviation industry is a world-leader: British Airways is one of the most profitable airlines in the world and BAA one of the few profitable airport operators

- 54 % of UK shipping revenues come from the highly competitive non UK-to-non UK markets; the world's second largest cruise company is British and the UK is among the world leaders in container operations and ferry services.

13 In domestic road distribution, the UK logistics sector also appears to perform well in comparison with similar firms in the other study countries (Exhibit 1):

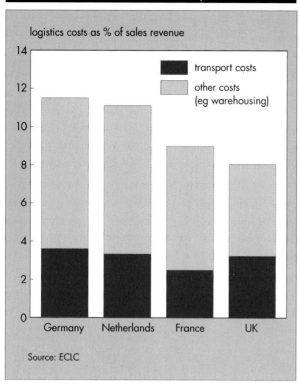

Exhibit 1 The UK distribution sector performs well

logistics costs as % of sales revenue

Source: ECLC

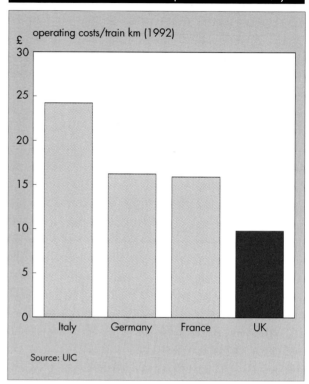

Exhibit 2 UK rail network is operated cost-effectively

operating costs/train km (1992)

Source: UIC

- Care has to be taken in interpreting these figures, given the many factors that need to be taken into account; for example, variations in the social costs to employers in different countries

- However, it is worth noting that the UK's apparent competitive edge comes wholly from the industry's ability to keep down its non-transport costs (such as those associated with warehousing): UK transport costs are on a par with those in Germany and the Netherlands and higher than in France.

14 The figures in Exhibit 1 also say little about the performance of the logistics sector in terms of time to markets, an increasingly important factor in product competitiveness. Time to market has increasingly influenced inward investors in Europe to base their distribution centres on the Continent. Dutch research on American and Japanese firms has shown that three out of four new European distribution centres set up in the last three years have been located in the Netherlands.

15 The UK also scores well in running railways cost-effectively (Exhibit 2). This reflects the efforts in recent years by British Rail to adopt a more commercial approach, within the context of Government policy generally to reduce the level of operating grants to the railways.

The quality of transport infrastructure

16 These relatively positive signs about the operation of transport services - albeit with some caveats - are not a reflection of the quality of UK infrastructure.

17 Clearly, experience will differ between various parts of the UK. In some cases - notably south-east England, the Midlands and the Central Belt in Scotland - congestion on various modes of transport is a greater issue than in more peripheral regions. In other cases, such as Northern Ireland, the lack of accessibility to markets is more of a concern.

Roads

18 The overall picture of the UK strategic transport network is that it is both less extensive and more congested than that of our main competitors. For example, the UK has among the most crowded roads in Europe (Exhibit 3). Figures for motorway traffic

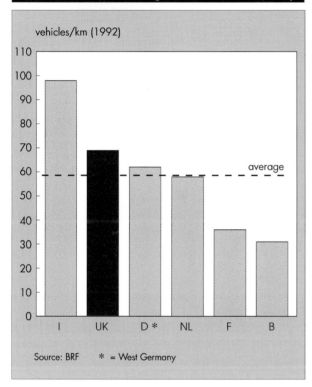

Exhibit 3 UK roads among the most crowded in Europe

vehicles/km (1992)

Source: BRF   * = West Germany

tell a similar story and are supported by the results of a recent British Road Federation study: 22% of the motorway network is currently operating above the capacity for which it was originally designed.

19 The inadequacy of the road network is of particular concern, given its importance, not just to business, but to the community as a whole (Exhibit 4). The performance of the network is likely to get worse as traffic levels increase. In particular, the forecast growth in car use represents the most significant challenge: cars and taxis already account for 82% of all motor traffic.

Exhibit 4 Road transport is the main mode in the UK

Freight Transport Percentage by mode (1993)		Passenger Transport Percentage by mode (1993)	
Road	63	Cars/vans	86
Rail	6	Buses/coaches	6
Water	25	Motor/pedal cycles	2
Pipeline	5	Rail	5
		Air	1

Source: DoT

Rail

20 The rail network in Britain is smaller per head of its population than those of its major European counterparts (Exhibit 5) - partly reflecting the relative sizes of the countries - although it does serve practically every significant conurbation, as well as many smaller ones.

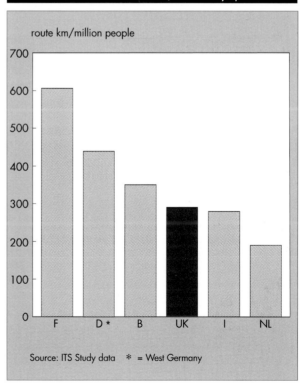

Exhibit 5 The UK rail network is relatively sparse....

route km/million people

Source: ITS Study data   * = West Germany

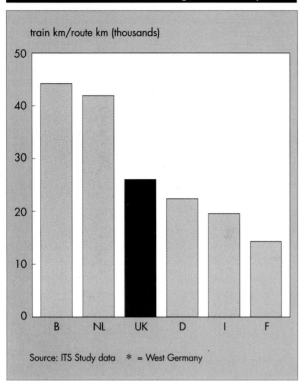

Exhibit 6 ...but has a medium-high traffic density

train km/route km (thousands)

Source: ITS Study data   * = West Germany

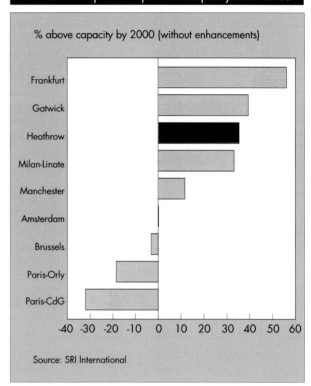

Exhibit 7 Major UK airports are capacity constrained

% above capacity by 2000 (without enhancements)

Source: SRI International

21 While the network is used relatively intensively (Exhibit 6), there is in general spare capacity available (with certain exceptions, eg commuter belts at peak times). However, notwithstanding recent improvements (e.g. to the East Coast Main Line), the failure to upgrade ageing infrastructure and rolling stock on parts of the network (e.g. the West Coast Main Line) will hamper the railways' attempts to compete successfully against other modes for more passenger and freight business.

Airports

22 Our leading airports, including Manchester, also face some of the severest constraints on capacity in Europe (Exhibit 7). The graph illustrates the extent to which capacity would be exceeded by the year 2000 were no enhancements put in place by then. Even though there are plans to develop UK airports (eg at Manchester and Heathrow), there are doubts about when, and even whether, such enhancements will be put in place. Yet other competing airports in Europe, such as Charles de Gaulle and Schiphol, are unlikely to face the same difficulties in completing their expansion plans.

Ports & Shipping

23 Nearly all of the UK's trade by volume passes through our ports. In recent years, more efficient working practices and access to private finance have enabled the ports to offer UK business a quality product.

24 In the case of UK shipping, however, there are causes for concern. The quality of shipping's capital assets - illustrated here in the worsening age-profile of the UK merchant fleet - raises questions about the sector's ability to maintain its competitiveness (Exhibit 8). Since 1980, the average age of the UK fleet has consistently been greater than that of the other study countries and, since the mid-1980s, higher than those the rest of the world.

Exhibit 8 The UK merchant fleet is getting older

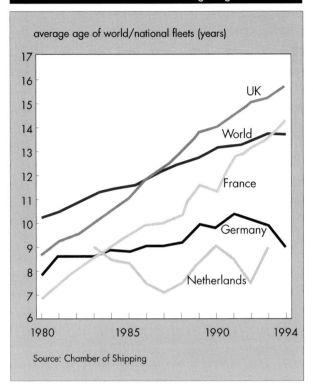

average age of world/national fleets (years)

Source: Chamber of Shipping

Exhibit 9 Road investment as a proportion of GDP (1985-91)

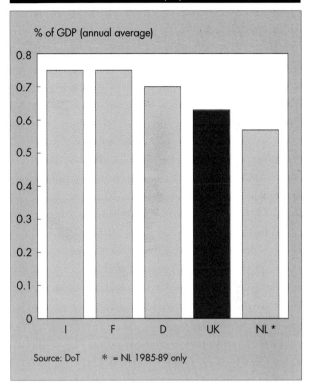

% of GDP (annual average)

Source: DoT * = NL 1985-89 only

Investment in infrastructure

25 In part, the constraints on our transport infrastructure reflect relatively low historic infrastructure investment. The figures used below are the latest which are readily available, although in some cases they do not cover the most recent years:

■ For roads, the figure is somewhat below those of major European competitors but that for rail is dramatically so (Exhibits 9-10)

■ In the case of airport investment, we have fared better (Exhibit 11) and since 1989, investment has continued, for example, in extra terminal capacity at Stansted and Manchester; yet the analysis above suggests that even here the UK has not kept pace with demand

■ The ageing of the UK merchant fleet can be linked to our comparatively poor record in investing in new ships (Exhibit 12). While investment in shipping is largely made by the private sector, the Government has a major influence in creating the climate for that investment.

Exhibit 10 Rail investment per head of population (1987-93)

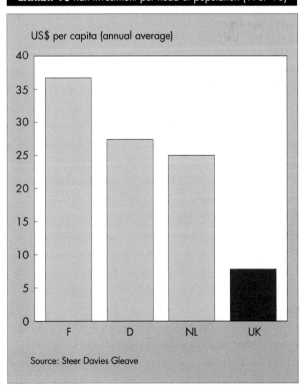

US$ per capita (annual average)

Source: Steer Davies Gleave

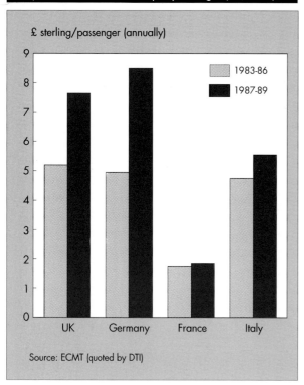

Exhibit 11 Air investment per passenger (1983-89)

£ sterling/passenger (annually)

Legend: 1983-86, 1987-89

Categories: UK, Germany, France, Italy

Source: ECMT (quoted by DTI)

Business views on the quality of transport links

26 The differences between countries in terms of the state of transport links is underlined by the generally more positive views which business people in other EU member states have about their networks.

27 Figures compiled for the World Economic Forum's 1994 Competitiveness Report (Exhibits 13-16) illustrate the extent to which different types of transport infrastructure meet business requirements, on a scale of one to ten.

28 These figures are based on the subjective assessments of business people surveyed in the individual countries and must be handled carefully, but they do suggest that:

■ The UK ranks in the bottom half of European Union member states on the quality of road and rail infrastructure

■ The UK ranks in the upper half on air infrastructure and access to ports

■ In the case of each of the four modes, the UK fares worse than our three other study countries.

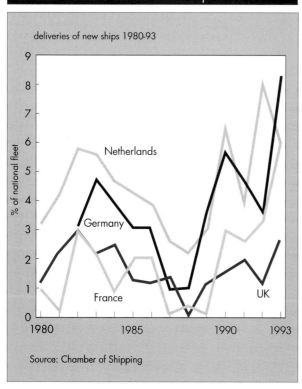

Exhibit 12 UK investment in new ships is low

deliveries of new ships 1980-93

% of national fleet

Netherlands, Germany, France, UK

Source: Chamber of Shipping

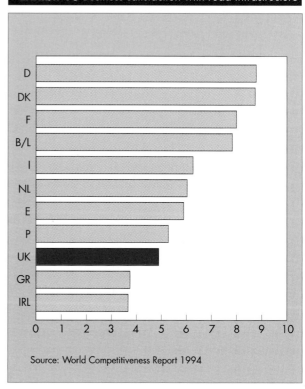

Exhibit 13 Business satisfaction with road infrastructure

Categories: D, DK, F, B/L, I, NL, E, P, UK, GR, IRL

Source: World Competitiveness Report 1994

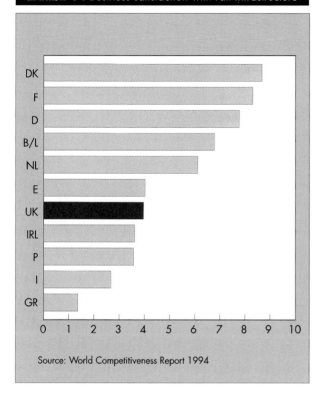

Exhibit 14 Business satisfaction with rail infrastructure

Source: World Competitiveness Report 1994

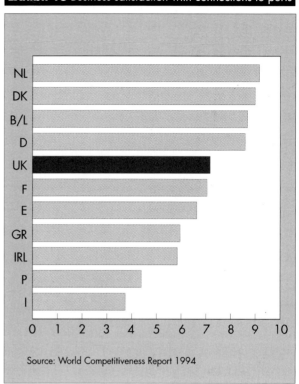

Exhibit 16 Business satisfaction with connections to ports

Source: World Competitiveness Report 1994

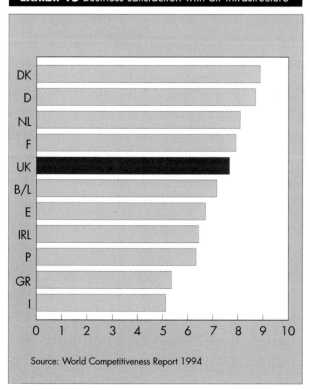

Exhibit 15 Business satisfaction with air infrastructure

Source: World Competitiveness Report 1994

29 The World Economic Forum graphs bear out the qualitative evidence provided by CBI interviews with French, German and Dutch businesses. Most organisations in these countries - unsurprisingly - said they would like current infrastructure plans to be implemented faster and investment levels increased. However, there was little sense of the urgency with which British businesses tend to view these matters.

30 Businesses in **the Netherlands** were most similar to the British in terms of concerns about congestion and under-investment; but there was a general sense that their Government had woken up to the problems and was seeking to improve matters.

31 In **Germany**, the general perception of the infrastructure was a good one, although it was recognised that much had to be done in the eastern half of the country. Concerns tended to focus more on the inefficient provision of services (rail freight services, for example, were criticised for their lack of focus on customer needs) and on the threat posed by future trends (eg the growth of transit traffic through Germany) rather than any legacy of past policy shortcomings.

32 In **France**, the quality of the national road network and of the still-developing TGV network were held in high regard; the latter was certainly seen as a symbol of national pride. Moreover, one opinion poll showed that whilst the vast majority of French citizens think they are affected by road congestion, only seven per cent are regularly caught in traffic jams.

Overall assessment

33 The current picture of the UK transport network, compared with that of some of our major European competitors, is a mixed one.

34 The relative strengths of the UK transport system - consistent with the liberalising emphasis of Government policy since the 1980s - lie in the competitiveness with which transport services are provided.

35 In addition, a recent KPMG survey of senior executives with foreign-owned companies based in the UK found that the UK's infrastructure and transport services were highly rated compared with their expectations (although these were not compared with expectations in other European countries).

36 But the relatively congested nature of the UK's transport infrastructure - explained at least in part by past under-investment - raises doubts about the extent to which the quality and efficiency of our domestic network and international links can be maintained.

37 In recent years, there has been some welcome recognition by the UK Government of the need to act. After a gradual fall in public spending on transport since the mid-1970s, expenditure has been rising since the late 1980s (Exhibit 17). However, the last two Budgets have cut planned transport expenditure: and although the Government is keen to attract more private investment in transport infrastructure, it remains to be seen to what extent the private sector will be willing to become involved.

38 Government policy on public spending is not the only constraint on improving the UK's transport network. Opposition to various road, rail, airport and port projects across the country is increasingly challenging the range of options open to the public and private sectors to build new capacity and enhance the quality of the old.

39 The debate about how far building new road capacity in particular can keep pace with future unconstrained demand has recently been fuelled by the SACTRA

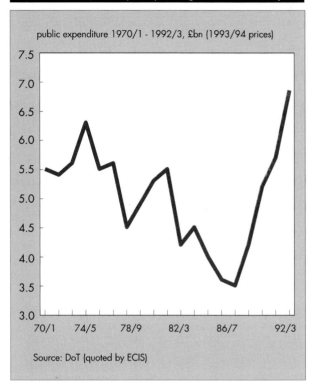

Exhibit 17 UK transport spending has risen recently

public expenditure 1970/1 - 1992/3, £bn (1993/94 prices)

Source: DoT (quoted by ECIS)

report. The danger is that this report will be seen wrongly by some groups as an excuse for doing nothing to improve the most important mode of transport for businesses and individuals alike.

40 At the same time, the debate on alternative courses of action - such as managing demand through price or, as is currently the case, through congestion - seems poorly informed and as yet too little attention has been paid to the likely impact of such measures on UK competitiveness.

41 The UK Government is not alone in facing these dilemmas and challenges. Governments in the other study countries are also trying to set transport policy which is environmentally sustainable and consistent with a general aim to control public spending. But the UK faces a particular challenge to its competitive position given its position on the periphery of Europe and the relatively poor quality of much of its existing infrastructure.

42 Successful national transport policy will increasingly involve difficult yet explicit choices about:

■ The level of demand for transport which is environmentally sustainable

■ The extent to which different types of transport demand - for example, passenger and freight - should have priority in using increasingly congested networks

■ How to provide adequate investment to support a desirable level of mobility

■ Modal priorities for investment and revenue support

■ How conflict can be avoided between measures to manage demand - where necessary - and business competitiveness.

43 Making the right policy choices is critical to the success of UK business in a competitive economy. The general political debate on UK transport policy is increasingly polarised between the "green" interest and the "transport" lobby. Trade-offs must, in fact, be made; the quality of life must be balanced against the need for growth and job creation built on internationally competitive businesses.

44 Countries which find the right trade-offs and invest for the long term are likely to be well-placed to secure a competitive edge over their rivals. The next section compares experience in the four study countries as to whether their decision-making structures meet this challenge.

Chapter 3

International experience

45 While the constraints facing European policy makers are in many cases the same, there are major differences in approach. In particular, transport policies in France, Germany and the Netherlands are characterised by three key strengths compared with UK experience.

46 First, while Governments in each of the study countries recognise they have a role in shaping transport policy, those in the Netherlands, Germany and France more explicitly set **strategic objectives** for policy.

47 Key features of this more strategic approach are:

■ A firm political recognition that providing good transport links is important in terms of broader policy objectives to encourage national economic development. In different ways, this is supported by the methods used to appraise investment in transport projects

■ More explicit policies, at least in principle in Germany and the Netherlands, to accommodate the forecast increase in traffic associated with economic growth in a sustainable manner.

48 Second, a broader political and public ownership of key strategic objectives, and how to address them, is fostered by a **more consensual policy making process**.

49 Third, there is **political long-term commitment to develop a high-quality transport infrastructure** which seeks to deliver agreed objectives.

50 However, there are also weaknesses in the way in which transport priorities are set in these countries. First, infrastructure schedule **plans have been known to fall behind** and Governments have in some cases failed to put politically difficult measures into effect.

51 Second, all four study countries are trying to reduce **perceived delay in their planning processes.**

52 Third, there is a general concern to control public spending and hence **interest in attracting private investment** in transport - but generally the record of other European countries on this **is less developed than in the UK.**

Key strengths in European transport policy-making

A strategic view of transport's economic importance

53 Governments in the four study countries all recognise that good transport links are economically important. However, there is a clear difference of emphasis between UK policy and that adopted in the three Continental countries.

54 For **the Netherlands**, whose economy is heavily dependent upon the success of its distribution sector, transport policy must serve the country's 'engines of growth' - the port of Rotterdam and Schiphol Airport. The view is that developing the country's links to European markets is essential if the Netherlands is not to become, in the words of one civil servant, 'the Jutland of Europe'.

55 The Dutch approach is exemplified by the activities of the Holland International Distribution Council. A non-profit organisation representing the interests of the transport and distribution industry, it is fully supported by the Dutch Government. Its aim is to promote the Netherlands as the gateway to Europe and as the ideal place for inward investors to locate their European distribution centres.

56 In **Germany**, Federal transport policy is substantially driven by their status as Europe's biggest transit nation. Thus 'German policy is at the same time European transport policy'. The country's infrastructure must be able to service the forecast growth in east-west traffic to prevent bottlenecks 'from inhibiting the economic development at a national and European level'.

57 There is also a wider social content to German transport policy. One of the main aims of Federal land use policy - to which transport planning is subordinate - is to create and maintain equivalent living conditions in all parts of Germany. The development of transport infrastructure is explicitly seen as part of policies for the spatial development of the country. Thus the current Federal infrastructure plan places much emphasis on developing links to and within the new Länder in the east.

58 In **France**, national infrastructure plans are also explicitly used alongside other tools of Government to pursue broader long-term economic aims. A key policy priority for the French Transport Ministry is to 'assert the position of France in European and world-wide competition'.

Exhibit 18 Transport and economic development in France

The development of transport links forms an integral part of the French Government's 'politique d'aménagement du territoire' - policies for the spatial development of the country's human, cultural and natural resources.

The aim of these policies is not simply to increase job creation, but also to develop a more cohesive society. The focus is very much upon enabling regions outside Paris to develop as areas of economic, educational and cultural activity in their own right, for example, by

■ Multiplying possible locations for industrial and social activity

■ Redeploying national administrative and technical functions to major cities, leaving Paris with the major sovereign functions and other activities needed to maintain its international attraction.

Two aspects are central to this approach:

■ A re-definition of the roles and funding of different levels of government, centred around greater participation by individuals in making decisions

■ Improved regional accessibility, with the State responsible for developing the major European routes and linking more peripheral regions to them.

Transport infrastructure is to serve a vision for the future development of France by:

■ Setting France at the heart of European growth by developing the Atlantic and Mediterranean seaboards as rivals to the 'blue banana' of economic growth from London to Milan

■ Changing the shape of transport links in France - with spokes currently radiating outwards from Paris - to enable French regions to be directly linked to their counterparts elsewhere in Europe.

This vision of the shape of France in 2015 represents the Government's contribution to a national debate on 'l'aménagement du territoire'. All French citizens have been invited to participate in this debate. The aim is to establish in law the principles by which the spatial development of the country will take place; this will in turn shape a national plan and regional plans below that.

Source: DATAR

---

59 The state has a clear vision of the spatial development of France in 20 years' time, and the role of transport infrastructure in supporting it (Exhibit 18). In the interests of social cohesion, the aim is to encourage the development of self-sustaining regions of economic activity, independent of Paris and competing with other

regions in Europe. Even so, there are still plans to improve transport links in Paris and the surrounding region.

60 While Governments in France, Germany and the Netherlands explicitly accept that they have a strategic role in transport, they are also looking to market forces to help provide a network which serves stated economic and social objectives. The French, for example have for many years contracted out the provision of transport services and infrastructure (see below on private finance).

61 National transport policy in **the UK**, by contrast, is less explicitly used by Government to promote strategic economic development. There is no clearly-stated vision of the spatial development of the country as a whole which the strategic transport network is to serve. The emphasis of UK policy lies instead in creating a market for transport with little explanation of the context - that is, the strategic policy aims - within which that market is to operate (Exhibit 19).

Exhibit 19 Strategic aims for the Department of Transport

The strategic policy aims for the Secretary of State for Transport are described in the Department of Transport's 1994 Report as:

The establishment of an efficient and competitive transport market to serve the interests of the economy and the community, with maximum emphasis on safety and the environment, achieved by:

■ Opening up new ways to make best use of private skills, initiative and funds

■ Providing substantial public sector investment, where appropriate

■ Getting better value for money from public expenditure on transport

■ Increasing competitiveness

■ Taking full account of the environmental implications of transport developments

■ Maintaining and, where necessary, improving transport safety

■ Using the price mechanism to give users and providers the right signals about the real costs of transport

■ Advancing UK transport interests in world markets.

Source: DoT

62 In addition - and in sharp contrast to the three Continental countries - the strategic aims of the Secretary of State for Transport do not refer to developing the UK's links to European markets. This should be a high priority for a country on the edge of the Single Market - the destination for over half the UK's exports.

63 The Government's record on integrating national transport priorities with proposals for trans-European networks (TENs) - one of whose aims is to help complete the Single Market - illustrate its relative lack of enthusiasm in taking a strategic view.

64 Many of the TEN routes affecting the UK actually identify existing strategic transport corridors. In practice, there is considerable overlap between national transport priorities and TEN development: for example, 64% by value of Priority 1 schemes in the English national roads programme will improve routes in the trans-European road network. Yet despite the UK's peripheral geography, the Government has been slow to ensure that plans for TENs give high priority to schemes improving the UK's access to the rest of Europe. Of the 34 TEN projects given priority status earlier in 1994, only three related to the UK.

65 However, there are some encouraging signs of Government recognition that it has a role to play in developing a good transport network to serve strategic economic aims:

■ The UK Government has subsequently lobbied both for the West Coast Main Line to be included in the list of priority projects and for one of the original three (Ireland-UK-Benelux road link) to be given a higher priority

■ National Government approves regional planning guidance, setting out a vision for the development of individual areas of the country and incorporating proposals for the development of transport infrastructure

■ Plans to develop the Thames Gateway emphasise the need for good transport infrastructure to be in place. One of the specific benefits of building the Channel Tunnel Rail Link will be 'to provide the impetus and development and regeneration of the Thames Gateway area, and East Kent, and assist Government's strategic planning objective of encouraging the movement of development pressure from west to east of London'

In the Scottish Office report for 1994, the Secretary of State states that further capital investment in roads and transport infrastructure - alongside health and education - is one of the priority areas of public spending which would be most effective in promoting long term growth and maintaining high standards of service to the public.

The Secretary of State for Wales is more direct in his appreciation of the importance of transport links:

■ 'Good transport brings jobs and investment. Manchester and Cardiff airports serve the North and South Wales business communities. Fast rail travel to London and beyond is an asset to Wales.'

Unlike the Department of Transport, both the Scottish and Welsh Offices put specific emphasis on economic regeneration as one of the objectives of the trunk roads programme.

While one of the aims of Government spending on English roads is generally 'to assist economic growth and efficiency by providing an effective road network',

■ In Scotland, apart from providing good inter-urban links and improving safety, one of the aims is to provide good accessibility to all other parts of the country 'where significant economic activity (including tourism) is carried on or could be expected to develop'

■ In Wales, assisting economic regeneration is a specific aim alongside other aims such as by-passing congested towns and improving road safety.

Source: Scottish Office, Welsh Office

■ The strategic transport aims for the Scottish and Welsh Offices (Exhibit 20) seem to give greater weight than the Department of Transport to the view that transport policy can serve as a tool of Government to encourage economic development. This in turn may at least in part be a reflection of the fact that the Scottish and Welsh Offices combine a number of Government functions and not just transport.

A strategic view of sustainable mobility: balancing economic and environmental objectives

66 Governments in each of the four countries assume that the demand for transport will continue to rise with economic growth. Each of them has also identified measures which aim to limit the environmental impact of such growth. But Germany and the Netherlands in particular, compared with the UK and France, have in place clearer national strategies to balance economic and environmental objectives for transport.

67 In practice, implementing such strategies can prove politically difficult (for example, see below on managing the demand for transport); but their existence provides a clear indication of the policy framework which the German and Dutch Governments feel is needed to deliver sustainable mobility.

68 The **Germans**, in developing their Federal transport infrastructure plan, have made transport policy a 'central plank' of their aim to reduce CO_2 emissions. An inter-ministerial working party has also been set up to address this issue. Official traffic forecasts covering all major modes (see also Exhibit 21 on the German approach to integrating modes) are based 'on assumptions of regulatory policy conditions, above all in view of the CO_2 reduction envisaged with (sic) the decision by the Federal Cabinet'.

69 German policy-makers argue that increasing the cost of transport - particularly road transport - is likely to be essential in reducing the environmental impact of transport. Yet in spite of the acknowledged difficulties of introducing such measures, this has not led to plans to stop increases in the capacity of transport infrastructure. Investment in infrastructure across all modes has been increased in current plans compared with previous years. These increases are seen as an important part of overall strategy to prevent forecast growth in traffic - for passengers and freight, across all modes - leading to gridlock.

70 The emphasis for German national transport policy remains on maintaining accessibility but in a more environmentally-sustainable way. As well as encouraging technical improvements to reduce the harmful effects of transport, there is a particular focus on encouraging a shift of traffic to more environmentally-friendly forms of transport, such as rail and inland waterways. Government is taking a lead, for example, by planning major investment to improve the railways; for the first time, there will be more new investment in rail than in roads.

71 Transport policy in **the Netherlands** is perhaps the most explicit in seeking to accommodate the growth in demand in a sustainable way. The same national policies - explicitly and jointly-owned by the Ministries responsible for Transport and Environment - designed to serve the 'engines of growth' also seek to achieve a number of specific environmental objectives.

72 These aims cover a wide range of areas, for example, reducing harmful emissions and noise pollution caused by transport. As in Germany, a mix of policy levers is seen as necessary to achieve environmental aims: improved technical standards, better public transport and links between modes, land use planning to reduce car use and pricing measures to 'adjust' the relative user costs of public transport and the private car in favour of the former.

73 These policies are not without critics. The VNO - the Dutch equivalent of the CBI - questions the extent to which economic and environmental objectives for transport policy can be achieved in practice. Proposed pricing measures to manage demand have also proved controversial.

74 However, transport policy in the Netherlands also leans heavily towards maintaining accessibility served by all modes. Although one aim is to reduce the rate of growth in road traffic, the assumption is that, as in the past, economic growth will lead to some increase in traffic which needs to be accommodated. Thus policy focuses on improving the performance of the road network (eg by policies to reduce the likelihood of congestion on the strategic network, including investment to remove bottlenecks) as well as investment in alternative forms of transport to encourage modal shift.

75 In **France**, there is no climate change programme, even though the French Government envoy signed the Rio Convention. There are policies to reduce the environmental effects of road transport (eg through particular emphasis on technical measures, but also through financial incentives to buy certain types of fuel and to trade in old vehicles for newer ones). However, there appears to be little concern generally with issues such as transport's contribution to global warming. Concern, such as it exists, tends to focus more on improving the safety record on roads and the local environmental effects of transport like noise.

76 In **the UK**, there have been recent signs that the Government is thinking more about the integration of environmental and transport policies. The Government's programme on climate change, for example, sets out initiatives to reduce CO_2 emissions from the transport sector. Planning policy guidance (PPG 13) produced jointly by the Departments of Transport and the Environment provides advice to local authorities on how integrating transport and land use planning could help to reduce reliance on the private car.

77 However, there is still a sense of tension between the Departments of the Environment and of Transport, most notably on the national roads programme. And the Treasury is effectively using current concern about the environment to increase the costs of transport (eg real term annual increases in fuel duty) without ploughing funds back in infrastructure investment to improve accessiblity.

78 The tension between departments is unlikely to be relieved by the recent SACTRA report on the traffic generated by new roads. In effect, the report bears out what policy-makers have already acknowleged: that new road capacity cannot be built to keep pace with all predicted traffic growth. In its 1990 document 'Trunk Roads, England: Into the 1990s', the Department of Transport said that the national roads programme was 'not intended to cater for all forecast demand to 2025. There will be cases where on economic and environmental grounds it is neither practicable nor desirable to meet the demand by road building, for example in city centres'.

79 It does not follow, however, that there should be neither any new capacity nor improvements to the existing network. But the absence of strategy has meant that there is no clear statement by Government on what it believes is needed to cope with that element of forecast demand which cannot be catered for through the roads programme, which in any event it has already cut several times.

80 Demand on parts of the network is effectively being rationed by the economically and environmentally inefficient tool of congestion. The Government's wish to see a shift of traffic from road to rail as one way of relieving pressure on the road network, for environmental reasons, is welcome and well-documented; but neither the size of shift which Government believes feasible is clear, nor the mix of policies needed to achieve it.

A strategic view of transport as a single market: the importance of a multi-modal approach

81 The difference of approach between Germany and the Netherlands on the one hand, and France and the UK on the other, in balancing economic with

environmental objectives, is underpinned by a greater willingness in the first two countries to see and develop transport networks as an integrated whole.

82 Policy **in Germany** in particular seeks to emphasise the complementary rather than the competitive relationship of different forms of transport (Exhibit 21). For example, Federal plans seek to develop high-speed rail links between airports as a way of reducing domestic air travel and so free airport capacity for international services. The development of combined transport terminals is also seen as a way of trying to encourage a shift of freight traffic away from road to rail.

83 Transport policy in **the Netherlands** also aims to improve links between different modes as part of overall policy to encourage a shift of traffic away from roads:

■ 'Full co-ordination' between the various sectors of the public transport system, and between public and private transport modes, is seen as vital to the policy aim of ensuring that home-to-work journeys by public transport on the main commuter routes take at most only 1.5 times longer than the same journeys by car (thus improving the attraction of public transport)

■ According to national policy (encapsulated in the SVV-II), long-distance rail travel can be encouraged if Europe's railways and airlines work together to co-ordinate their services, freeing airport capacity for inter-continental traffic

■ By 2000, 'all parts of the country, and in particular the port areas' are to be served by road, waterway and rail terminals.

84 In addition, funding for transport in the Netherlands has been reformed to provide a better framework for operating an integrated transport policy. Since January 1994, a new Infrastructure Fund has been in place (see paras 129-131). This aims to bring greater coherence to the different streams of income for the Ministry of Transport to enable 'financial and substantive priorities to be set in more coherent fashion, allowing the relative merits of spending on different types of infrastructure to be assessed and helping to optimise the managment and use of available resources' (though note that airport, port and inland waterway infrastructure are not covered by the Fund).

Exhibit 21 Integrating different transport modes: the German approach

The thrust of the Federal Traffic Infrastructure Plan of 1992 (BVWP 92) is to facilitate the mobility "needed by the Federal Republic of Germany as a location of economic activities" in a way that is compatible with environmental and social concerns.

While the BVWP 92 proposes substantial investment in all modes, including roads, one of its cornerstones is to improve integration between different transport modes. This is seen as

'the only recognisable chance of freeing ourselves in conformity with market conditions from the one-sided growth which has concentrated on road and air transport'.

For the Federal Transport Ministry, there are three important instruments underpinning this approach:

■ Integrated overall traffic forecasts for all modes, covering passenger and goods transport. They assume, for example, a probable increase in the costs of transport to the user and the effects on road transport of constraints on capacity combined with improvements to rail transport

■ The use of uniform criteria for appraising investment in road, rail and inland waterway projects (see Exhibit 26)

■ An enhanced role for information technology, supported by Federal funding of over DM 6 billion for road and rail IT projects to the year 2010 and beyond.

To improve the interfaces between modes and encourage a shift of traffic away from road and air in particular, the BVWP lists a number of possible proposals to

■ Integrate the country's airports more fully into the high speed rail network, not only to attract long-distance feeder road traffic onto rail, but also to shift traffic from domestic air routes to rail, thus freeing airport capacity for long-haul flights

■ Develop a network of combined transport terminals to attract freight traffic away from road to rail, at a cost of some DM 4 billion: finance could be made available from Federal funds. These terminals would offer scope for co-ordinated deliveries to town centres, further reducing road traffic

■ Support improved links to sea and inland ports with Federal funds.

Source: BVWP 92

---

85 The importance given to co-ordinating policies, not only for different modes but between countries, is emphasisied in a statement on short-sea shipping prepared jointly in June 1994 between the Transport Ministers of Belgium, Germany and the Netherlands. The tendency to see shipping as an isolated sector is

seen as a reason why its potential as an alternative to other modes has been under-estimated in the past. The statement ends by saying that 'transport policy should, like transport itself, be increasingly characterised by an integrated multimodal approach both nationally and internationally. Such an approach is essential to ensure efficient handling of freight traffic in the future while minimising pollution and improving safety. This calls for co-ordination among the various authorities and co-opertaion between Government and industry.'

86   The picture in **France** is different, certainly at the national level. Policy appears less concerned with achieving modal shift - the low density of land use in France makes it relatively easier in many cases to provide new capacity to meet demand - and more with improving the overall level of access.

87   Thus development of the TGV network appears less as a means of taking traffic away from air travel and more as a means of improving links to regions. This policy can in some cases lead to over-provision of capacity (such as the Route des Estuaires in the north-west) to meet strategic aims of 'unlocking' the potential of regions (desenclavement) rather than simply to meet expected demand.

88   Nevertheless, improved links between modes - such as the inclusion of Charles de Gaulle airport on the TGV network - is still seen as desirable in terms of improving overall accessibility. Plans for a north-south 'autoroute ferroviare', which would carry HGVs by rail, have also recently been revived. And national Government has become concerned about the failure of some towns to see local transport networks as a coherent whole (for example, some have invested in expensive public transport systems more for prestige rather than as part of broader policies to encourage modal shift away from cars in urban areas).

89   The position in **the UK** contrasts with the position in Germany, for example, where the Federal Government sees a direct role for itself in developing an integrated transport network. The thrust of the UK Government's approach is that the market and not the Department of Transport should determine how and where integration of modes should take place.

90   The relative unwillingness of Government to date to approach transport nationally on a multimodal basis is illustrated in various ways:

■ Heathrow - the world's premier international airport - remains unconnected to the national railway network; even when the Heathrow Express is completed, it will provide a fast link to the centre of London only (although BAA is now looking at the scope for additional rail links to Heathrow)

■ The recent decision to restrict the economic and environmental benefits of 44 tonne lorries to railhead operations alone is all the more limited in that it does not extend to other intermodal operations, namely to and from ports.

91   The Government's willingness to promote integration even within one mode has not always been obvious. Plans for rail privatisation originally did not see the need for some sort of guarantee for things like through-ticketing or, in London, the Travelcard. The rationale was that it would probably be in the commercial interest of rail operators in any event to ensure the continued existence of these. Uncertainty that this would in fact happen led the government to include re-assurances to the contrary in its proposals, although even these have recently been brought into question.

92   However, there have been some encouraging developments:

■ In the past, the DoT had been organised on a modal basis: this was widely criticised as an obstacle to the development of multi-modal policy. That has recently changed so that the DoT is now divided into two main sections - one for infrastructure and one for the operation of services - in which all modes are handled

■ While the Government itself does not develop a multi-modal transport strategy - national road proposals are developed separately from those for rail, and those in turn are developed separately from those for air and maritime operations - it specifically encourages local authorities to do so (and to prepare such proposals where necessary with other local authorities) in bidding for central Government grants

■ Government reforms to the railway include an extended grants scheme (eg for buidling intermodal terminals) to encourage a shift of freight traffic from road to rail.

The importance of consensus

93 The Secretary of State for Transport has recently illustrated both the importance of building consensus on policy objectives, and the current lack of it in the UK.

94 Seeking consensus does not mean removing debate. It is the process through which the different stakeholders in society - national and local Government, business, the general public - all feel that they are taking part, in a meaningful way, in the identification and selection of policy choices.

95 The value of such a process is to broaden ownership of the problems and solutions in transport policy-making. This is vital in encouraging continuity of policy and a stable framework within which business can confidently plan ahead. But it cannot be seen as a substitute for firm action by Government.

96 The lack of consensus in the UK is another relative weakness in our decision-making process compared with France, Germany and the Netherlands. It would be idle to pretend that there are no differences of opinions in those countries: but there are numerous mechanisms through which a broader public understanding and acceptance of policy issues is built. Three areas are particularly noteworthy.

Exhibit 22 A move towards consensus?

'I wish to see an end to the shouting and insults - sometimes even the actual violence - that have characterised arguments about transport in recent years.

'I want a ceasefire; a fresh start. We need to move back to properly-informed, rational argument, with respect for opposing views, in a manner more fitting to the democratic traditions of our country.

'My aim is to define the questions and seek to pose them in as sharp and clear a way as possible. I hope others will contribute to that process and, more importantly, will then help shape the answers to those questions.'

Dr Brian Mawhinney, 7 December 1994

The role of regional government

97 In general, regional/local Government in the Continental countries has a greater role in shaping and delivering transport policies than in the UK. This is frequently underpinned by greater financial independence in general for lower tiers of Government on the Continent (Exhibit 23).

Exhibit 23 Local Government funding in Europe

Percentage of local Government revenue
derived from other levels of Government (1992)

France	36.8
Germany (1991) - state, region or province	17.0
- local	27.5
Netherlands	71.5
United Kingdom	70.3

Source: IMF

---

98 In **Germany**, the national infrastructure plan is brought before parliament, debated and agreed. Given the federal nature of the German constitution, this arrangement also gives state Governments a role in ratifying national policy.

99 In addition to this, state Governments have relative freedom in deciding how to use money made available to them by the Federal Government for local public transport and road construction. While Federal Government retains responsibility for local rail projects of major importance, the Länder can now use Federal aid flexibly 'for promotable projects according to their own concepts'.

100 In **France**, the country's 22 regions enter into five-year contracts with national Government to develop transport infrastructure as a means of promoting regional development. This is buttressed by the growth in regional financial power over the last decade or so. Regions are also able to enter into similar contracts with other regions, as is the case with the eight regions in the Paris Basin.

101 The links between French policy-making at national and lower levels are underpinned by another factor. Ninety per cent of senators, for example, simultaneously hold senior positions in local politics.

102 In **the Netherlands**, there has been little past emphasis on developing transport policy at a regional level. In

addition, local Government has relatively little financial independence to act. However, it can be argued that the size of the country is such that it does not make sense for central government to devolve much power to lower levels of government.

103 Even so, transport policy in the Netherlands is currently undergoing some change with a centrally-driven policy to encourage the establishment of 'Transport Regions'. These would be responsible at a regional level for preparing and implementing transport policy in co-ordination with land use planning. The aim is to improve co-ordination amongst local authorities and between municipalities, provincial and central Government. Central Government is hoping to encourage action with the promise of bundling specific-purpose funds together, allowing a more flexible deployment of resources in the region.

104 In the **UK**, there is little scope for local Government to influence the setting of national transport priorities and hence to share in ownership of policy. This is exacerbated by the lack of effective representation at a regional level of local concerns and in particular the limits on the financial power of local Government.

105 The relative failure of local and central Governments to talk to each other has led to some notable difficulties for the execution of transport policy. The Department of Transport came under severe criticism earlier this year from local authorities for including a Felixstowe-Fishguard route in the trans-European road network (TERN) plans. The affected local authorities claimed not to have been consulted on the scheme; and the route was subsequently dropped from the TERN plans. The Scottish Office was also criticised last year for failure to include a number of routes in the TERN proposals: additions have subsequently been made.

106 Nevertheless, there are positive signs:

- Regional planning conferences have been set up around the country, often taking a lead from SERPLAN in the South East, to provide a forum for discussion within which interested bodies, including the business community, can formulate a vision for the development of transport policy for a region. However, such conferences lack any financial resource to implement this vision

- Successful lobbying of the DoT by local authorities to enable them to submit package bids for Government grants illustrates the willingness of both central and local Government to work together in developing local multi-modal transport strategies.

In metropolitan areas, PTAs and PTEs have been active in delivering such strategies at a local level.

- The recent establishment of integrated regional offices (IROs) of Whitehall departments may yet prove a useful channel for local interests to communicate their concerns to central Government. It may also enable further integration at a regional level of transport policy with other public policy objectives.

- The SACTRA report noted that in preparing trunk road schemes in Scotland (and so, implicitly, not elsewhere in the country), relevant local authority objectives are incorporated into scheme objectives.

Business involvement in the decision-making process

107 In France and the Netherlands, the existence of semi-official bodies provide useful channels through which business can take part in the setting of priorities. In **the Netherlands**, the willingness of the business community to see itself as an active player extends to the initiative - with Government support - to develop company transport plans as a means of reducing the environmental impact of transport.

108 In addition, a forum for debate exists in the form of a tripartite socio-economic advisory council made up of representatives from government, academics/other individuals and representatives from both employers and unions. The issues to be debated by the council can be determined either by ministers or the other partners in the group.

109 This council appears to have influence. In 1986, the unions and employers agreed that the Dutch Government needed to place greater emphasis on improving infrastructure: one commentator believed that this was instrumental in bringing about the Government's initial proposals for the Second Transport Structure Plan (SVV-II).

110 In **France**, there are advisory bodies to regional government: eg in Basse-Normandie the Conseil Economique et Social Régional (CESR), which advises the Conseil Régional on planning and other matters. This body is made up of representatives from various organisations (eg employers and unions) as well as of elected representatives.

111 The involvement of the business community also takes another form through the activities of the Chambers of Commerce, some of whom are responsible for the operation of transport infrastructure, eg ports, airports.

Public consultation on important policy issues

112 Public participation in policy formulation is a key facet of national transport policy in **the Netherlands**. Current policy, encapsulated in the Second Structure Plan (SVV-II), was put out to public consultation prior to being finalised by Government. The final document refers to the fact that 'no policy proposals have ever elicited such a massive response'.

113 Civil servants from the Transport Ministry have also acknowledged, given the military origins of their department, that little effort has been spent in the past on cultivating a good image with the general public.

114 This is seen as a weakness and is being reversed. One specific aim of policy is to enhance public understanding of the purpose of the SVV-II. The key issue to be dealt with is 'the Dutch public's increasing recognition that continued growth in mobility will face us with almost insuperable problems in the areas of accessibility and quality of life'.

115 Since the plan was agreed, official surveys have been carried out to establish the public's response to policies. A review of the SVV-II by the Transport Ministry in December 1993 claimed that almost all of the public were fully familiar with the broad outlines of the SVV-II; and that in practice the level of public support for it was 'much greater' than assumed by politicians.

116 It should also be noted that **in France**, the debate on the future shape and development of the country is one which the Government has openly encouraged all citizens to take part.

117 In **the UK**, there is no overall policy for transport which is presented for public consultation and then agreed in Parliament. For example, the roads programme is effectively determined by the Department of Transport and then presented without debate as the Government's programme (which, in any event, it has failed to keep to).

118 Mechanisms for consultation do exist, such as Green Papers. The Government recently chose to use this approach, but to generate debate on its plans for motorway charging, rather than on transport policy as a whole. Even its original proposals for rail privatisation were published as a White Paper and thus as a formal statement of policy rather than as a Green Paper.

Long term transport programmes supported by financial commitment

119 With greater public understanding of objectives and policies, it becomes easier for Governments to build long-term commitment to improve their transport infrastructure. France, Germany and the Netherlands each have detailed long-term infrastructure plans, some extending as far as 20 years ahead (Exhibits 24-25).

Exhibit 24 Planned investment in German Federal transport infrastructure 1991-2010

	DM billions	% of total investment
Rail:		
new construction	108.3	
replacement/other investment	86.8	
	194.9	39.5
Road:		
new construction	99.6	
replacement/other investment (not maintenance)	91.8	
	191.4	38.8
Waterways:		
new construction	14.7	
replacement/other investment	13.3	
	28.0	5.7
Federal aid for local public transport/road construction:	76.1	15.4
Miscellaneous:	2.6	0.6
Total Investment:	493.0	100.0
of which new construction:	(222.6)	(42.0)

Source: BVWP 92

Exhibit 25 Planned transport expenditure in the Netherlands 1991-2010

	bn guilders	capital spending (bn guilders)
Trunk roads:		
construction/ utilisation	18.4	
tunnels (private finance)	2.0	20.4
maintenance	17.2	
	37.6	
Road safety/cycling infrastructure:	2.8	2.8
Urban traffic scheme grants:	2.1	
Railways/other collective transport:		
investment	29.6	29.6
operations	84.4	
	114.0	
Waterways:		
construction	4.0	4.0
maintenance	6.3	
	10.3	
Incentives: eg IT, combined transport, inflencing behaviour	1.6	
Research:	1.0	
Total Expenditure:	169.4	
of which capital spending:		56.8
		(33.5 % of total spending)

Source: SVV-II

120 Each of the three Continental countries also use five-year financial planning windows. While all Governments' investment plans are subject to annual budgets, there is general confidence on the Continent that long-term commitments will be met. Of particular note is the fact that in each of the three Continental countries, current spending plans represent substantial increases on past plans.

121 In **Germany**, the current Federal Transport Infrastructure Plan (BVWP '92) proposes average annual investment of DM 24.6 billion per annum, compared with DM 12.6 billion - for West Germany - in the previous plan (BVWP '85). It is also worth noting that:

■ While planned investment in all modes has increased, the share of total investment has moved in favour of rail: for the first time, more will be invested in the railways (40%) than in roads (under 39%)

■ The BVWP 92 spending plans include 60 billion DM for 'backlog' projects (for example, completion of schemes already underway and those agreed as necessary in 1990 to link the eastern and western German transport networks.

122 In **France**, projected total investment in the current five-year period (1994-98) represents a 42% increase over out-turn in the previous five years. In his November 1993 budget, the Transport Minister authorised the autoroute concessionaires to raise additional funds over the period 1994-2003 to bring forward by five years the completion of the remaining 3000 kms of the autoroute programme.

123 In **the Netherlands**, the spending plans set out in the SVV-II marked a significant increase over the Government's initial proposals. Some of the extra spending was re-allocated from other sectors (for example, there was a considerable reduction in spending on road construction and widening compared with the initial proposals). Other instruments envisaged included the introduction of a peak-hour surcharge in the Randstad on vehicle tax and the funding of new tunnels in the Randstad through tolls.

124 However, partly due to escalating costs, the Netherlands Government realised that the SVV-II spending plans would not be enough to meet policy objectives. Thus the Government has decided to make available an additional 5 billion guilders for 1994-1998, increasing the annual transport budget by 14% to 9.4 billion guilders in 1998 (c. 45% of which will be for infrastructure investment).

125 By contrast, in **the UK**, there is no similar, multi-modal long-term programme. There is a recently-reviewed roads programme worth £18 billion that has no definitive completion date. Railtrack is also due to prepare a ten-year investment programme in rail infrastructure: British Rail in 1991 produced its own proposed agenda for the decade (Future Rail), but that was not followed up by Government.

126 Financial planning in the UK takes place over three years; but experience has not generated confidence that Government investment will either make up ground lost in the past or be sustained. Despite a rise in spending on transport in recent years, current plans indicate a cut in the DoT's budget. In addition:

■ Despite the recent re-prioritisation of the roads programme in spring 1994 - which also included cuts - the DoT's roads budget was cut again in the November 1994 Budget; and the SACTRA report may further threaten the programme

■ The Government's agreement in 1991 that increased levels of investment were needed in London Underground was soon undermined by subsequent cuts in public funding for investment in the Tube network

■ Where long-term commitment does take place, it tends to be on a project-by-project basis rather than within the context of an overall strategy to deliver improvements (eg annual uncertainty about which of the various light rail projects around the country will receive funding). Moreover, the extent of Government commitment to individual projects such as CrossRail or the Channel Tunnel Rail Link can tend to blow hot and cold.

127 In some cases on the Continent, the greater sense of stability afforded by longer-term financial planning is underpinned by some ring-fencing of revenues specifically for transport improvements.

128 In **Germany**, a small proportion (5%) of revenue from fuel duty (mineralölsteuer) is dedicated by the Federal Government to supporting local transport policies.

This in turn accounts for 50 per cent of Federal transport aid to the Lander.

129 In **the Netherlands**, a new Infrastructure Fund was set up in January 1994. It aims to bring together, under a single budget, different sources of public funding specifically for transport infrastructure. For 1994-1998, this fund breaks down as follows:

■ 2 billion guilders per annum from the supplement on motor vehicle tax

■ 0.9 billion guilders from duty on motor fuel

■ 2.3 billion guilders from general resources

■ 0.5 billion guilders from natural gas revenues (for a high-speed passenger rail link and the Betuwe rail freight link)

■ 0.9 billion guilders from the investment round (sic).

130 An important facet of this fund is that any underspend does not go back to Government coffers. This has actually led to a situation - now being rectified - in Rotterdam where delays in the preparation of schemes mean that the local authority is currently unable to spend its full allocation!

131 It is also important to note that certain elements of the Infrastructure Fund (eg that part made up of gas revenues) has been set up as a joint initiative between the Dutch equivalents of the UK's Treasury and DTI. This is dedicated to infrastructure developments which are seen as assisting the country's economic development.

132 In **France**, the 'versement transport' - a levy on employers over a certain size - is dedicated to funding public transport in Paris and other major cities.

133 In **the UK**, the Treasury has proved itself hostile to the idea of ring-fencing revenue from transport-related taxation to transport improvements (although originally road tax revenue was hypothecated). More recently, however, the Government has acknowledged in its proposals for motorway charging that the proceeds should be ploughed back into improving the network.

The use of multi-criteria analysis for investment appraisal

134 At one level, similar investment appraisal methods are used by the study countries to decide which projects should go ahead. However, important differences of emphasis between practice in the UK and that on the Continent underpin the more strategic view in France, Germany and the Netherlands of the role of transport.

135 Both financial appraisal (comparing the revenues generated and financial costs incurred by a project) and a broader, economic appraisal (comparing all benefits and costs, to users and non-users) have a place in the appraisal processes of each country. The latter is used in each country for road investment, while financial evaluation is often used for rail projects.

136 However, there are some notable differences in approach. In **Germany**, economic evaluation is used at the Federal level not just for roads, but for rail, and inland waterway schemes as well: for rail, 'operational efficiency' of a measure is 'indispensable'. Economic evaluation is also used for both road and rail in the **Netherlands**.

137 In **France**, rail projects with a <u>financial</u> rate of return of at least 8% are taken forward by SNCF; those which do not meet this criteria, but which have an <u>economic</u> rate of return of at least 8%, proceed with financial support from the State.

138 In **the UK**, economic evaluation is used at a national level for road but not rail schemes. Prior to the Railways Act, the key requirement for investment in InterCity and freight services was an 8% financial rate of return; for grant supported services (eg Regional Railways) and urban/local rail schemes, financial appraisal was a key consideration, although cost-benefit analysis could also be used to assess wider benefits arising from such investment.

139 Where economic evaluation of a project is carried out, the use of cost-benefit analysis (CBA) to compare a project's costs and benefits (expressed in monetary terms) is important to all the study countries. In fact, CBA is often but one of a number of factors considered within broader types of multi-criteria analysis (MCA) in deciding whether a scheme should proceed:

- In **Germany**, CBA is set alongside other criteria which cannot adequately be valued in monetary terms but which are seen as important to the decision-making process (Exhibit 26). Criteria which

support a strategic vision are thus formally and clearly included in appraising projects: for example, the German concept of an integrated, multimodal network is underpinned by assessing, where appropriate, the interdependence of road and rail, and by the very fact that the same assessment methodology (ie economic evaluation) is used for all major modes

- In the **Netherlands**, a formal MCA is used to rank projects in terms of their relative priorities: the criteria used depend on current policies and are derived from the SVV-II. Five broad criteria categories are considered and each is weighted (out of 100) to reflect its importance to decision-makers:

economic activity (limited CBA)	35
road safety	20
human environment (noise/air pollution)	25
transit role (importance for freight)	15
physical planning (impact on land use)	5

- In **France**, ten criteria are considered in the economic evaluation of road schemes, including the results of monetary CBA, environmental impacts (mainly qualitative measures), the impact of a scheme in regional/local economic development and the effect on other modes

- In **the UK**, CBA and environmental assessment are the key factors in determining the investment case for trunk road schemes. The 1994 roads review revealed that, in practice, a broader methodology is used. Other factors considered are the importance of a scheme as part of the trunk road network, 'special local considerations' and priorities for public policy (eg building urgently-needed bypasses).

140 A key difference in approach appears to be that the more formal use of MCA on the Continent provides a basis for making investment decisions which is more transparent than that in the UK. Indeed, transparency of decision-making is specifically emphasised in the German methodology: viz, an explanation has to be provided in cases where the ranking of a scheme in the Federal plan is changed, for example, for environmental reasons.

Exhibit 26 Federal transport investment appraisal in Germany

All major Federal infrastructure projects, covering road, rail and waterways, are assessed according to comparable criteria. The criteria considered fall into four broad categories, none of which is given absolute priority. Due to their inherent differences, these factors are not combined to form a single assessment factor, but are summarised in a uniform manner to aid decision-making on which projects should go ahead, and with what degree of priority.

Economic assessment
The costs of building, operating and maintaining a scheme are assessed against the following benefits:

■ Operating cost savings and improvement in accessibility

■ Benefits for regional development, including the effects of employment during construction and employment

■ Improved traffic safety

■ Reduced noise and air pollution, particularly in the case of local bypasses.

Ecological Assessment
A general ecological risk analysis is carried out: more detailed assessment (for example, on the balance between loss of amenity and compensation replacement measures) only occurs at later, subsidiary stages.

At the Federal planning stage, therefore, it is not normally possible to say whether or not a scheme is environmentally compatible. However, if there are many ecological problems without any prospect of effective remedial measures, a scheme can be given a lower priority or dropped altogether. But, if, after consideration of all factors, priority is given to the transport policy objective of a scheme, although considerable environmental problems have been recognised, the scheme is not downgraded. The environmental problems have instead to be dealt with within the framework of further planning.

Town planning assessment (federal trunk roads only)
This is limited to projects where significant effects (within a range of 10 Km to both sides) are expected due to traffic reductions (30% or more) or traffic increases (50% or more). The effects considered include impacts on the arrangement of urban spaces, amenity of places and severance.

Additional criteria
The above categories are supplemented, where relevant, by

statements on, for example,

■ The interdependence of road and rail on inter-urban and urban corridors: this is examined where significant modal shift has been forecast. While it is envisaged that this will increase the attractiveness of rail schemes, it does not preclude the possibility that parallel road and rail projects might proceed rather than just the latter

■ Integration of combined transport facilities and goods distribution centres

■ Political agreements with neighbouring countries

■ Projects of outstanding importance (for example, if they are the only efficient link which an area will have, either internationally or domestically).

Discount rate
To calculate the net present value of a scheme, the future flow of costs and benefits is discounted at a rate of 3%. This is used on the basis of the expected real national rate of economic growth.

Prioritisation of projects
Schemes in the Federal infrastructure plan are divided into projects of first and second priority. The investment programme for the current plan covers the projects of first priority (including schemes from the previous plan and new measures subsequently deemed necessary, for example, to support reunification); second priority schemes fall outside this financial frame but are still deemed to be of overall economic benefit.

New projects are prioritised on the following basis:

■ Cost/benefit ratio: if it is greater than 3, schemes are eligible for first priority and if it is at least 1, for second priority

■ Ecological assessment at the Federal level must already show that later planning stages will provide an ecologically acceptable alignment if it is to achieve first priority status: otherwise it will be downgraded or dispensed with

■ The results of town planning and additional criteria assessment.

Source: Federal Ministry of Transport

141 Finally, it is worth noting that the types of economic evaluation used on the Continent explicitly (yet in different ways) place more emphasis on the perceived wider economic benefits of transport investment than does the DoT:

■ In **Germany**, the 3% discount rate used to calculate a scheme's net present value yields a higher value

for money than would the 8% discount rate used by the DoT. The rationale for the German rate - based on the expected real national rate of economic growth - seems to be that any consumption foregone (by investing in a project) in a particular year should achieve at least as much growth as in the general economy

■ The methodology used in **the Netherlands** places substantial weight not just on economic activity but also on the importance of a route in serving freight traffic

■ Appraisal in **France and Germany** - unlike the UK - includes some formal assessment of the impact of a scheme on regional economic development.

The use of targets to measure the success of transport policies in meeting objectives

142 Targets to measure the performance of public policies are used in each of the study countries. Generally speaking, targets are used less as objectives which must be achieved at any cost and more as an aid to policy-making on the effectiveness of allocating resources, though there are differences in the importance attached to the targets adopted.

143 Transport policy in **the Netherlands** sees the greatest use of targets as a yardstick against which the performance of policies can be measured (Exhibit 27). The range of policy areas - economic and environmental - is unrivalled in the other study countries. It should be noted that not all targets are being met; but this failure itself informs decision-makers on how policies need to be fine-tuned or changed.

144 Target setting is also evident to some degree in **Germany**:

■ Scenarios of future traffic growth, comparing do-minimum approaches with what is desirable/possible, rather than targets per se, are used to inform national policy making

■ There are targets for CO_2 emission reduction: transport policy plays a significant part in seeking to achieve those targets

■ Targets for modal split are used at a local level. At the national level, the Federal Transport Minister has said that he wants to see a 10% shift in traffic from road to rail.

145 In **France**, there is little evidence of the use of targets as such, but performance of policies is in a sense monitored through the contractual system of delivering policy objectives.

146 Target-setting is also used in **the UK** (for example, on stabilising CO_2 emissions, reducing road accident casualties and in the form of the Passengers' Charter

---

Exhibit 27 Dutch transport policy and the measurement of performance

The Second Transport Structure Plan (SVV-II) states that it is not enough for transport strategy to 'stick at the stage of expressing serious concern and pious wishes'.

The SVV-II therefore draws up a host of target scenarios within the four main policy categories. Some of the targets used are specific, while others are less precise; sometimes there is also a distinction between the short and long-term (eg scenarios for 1995 and 2010):

■ Policy Category 1: Environment and amenity

- In 2010, CO_2 emissions from road vehicles to be 10 per cent lower than in 1986

■ Policy Category 2: Managing mobility

- Reducing the rate of forecast growth in road traffic over the period 1986-2010 from 72% to 35%

■ Policy Category 3: Accessibility

- by 2010, there will be a 2% probability of congestion on main road links to Rotterdam and Schiphol, and 5% on other parts of the trunk road network

- the Netherlands' share in international freight traffic will at least be maintained

■ Policy Category 4: Support measures

- by 1995, all businesses and Government institutions with more than 50 employees will have a company transport plan

Two years after the publication of the SVV-II, the Ministry of Transport conducted a review of the Plan. Some of its conclusions were that:

■ Society is now even more aware that a policy on vehicle use must be pursued

■ While the restriction on traffic growth has been proceeding as expected when the SVV-II was compiled, the long-term targets will not be reached unless planned large rises in the cost of road use are implemented

■ The positive effects of improvements to public transport have been counter-balanced by fare increases

■ The problem of road congestion as a whole continues to increase, despite improvements to some bottlenecks and is likely to overshoot targets unless 'policy is modified on a number of points'.

Source: Ministry of Transport, Public Works and Water Management

for rail services. However, there are instances at the strategic and tactical level where targets are not currently used but which might strengthen policy making:

■ At the strategic level, although the government has said it wants to see a shift of traffic from road to rail, it has not given any indication of the extent to which it believes this desirable or achievable

■ At the tactical level, targets have not yet been set for performance of the trunk road network. However, the Highways Agency is committed to providing these by April 1995; the recent establishment of a Road Users' Committee is a welcome development which should help this initiative.

Key weaknesses in European transport policy-making

Managing the demand for transport

147 There is a growing acceptance in the four countries - perhaps with the exception of France, where constraints on space and concerns about the environment are less of a political issue - that new transport infrastructure, and in particular road infrastructure, cannot be built to keep up with forecast demand. Although there have long been measures at urban level to deal with this problem using a mix of policy levers, there is growing interest in policies (especially use of pricing measures) on a larger scale.

148 The **German** Government has recognised that massive increases in the cost of road use might be effective but are politically unacceptable. Recent proposals to introduce electronic charging for motorways - technology trials are already under way - have encountered stiff public opposition. The emphasis of national policy is thus to encourage a shift of traffic away from road and air to the railways through specific policies, for example, to improve the links between those forms of transport.

149 Transport policy in **the Netherlands** in theory places great emphasis on increasing the cost of road use - alongside improvements to public transport - as a means of halving the forecast increase in road traffic from 72% to 35% by the year 2010. 70% of the effects of policies to achieve a reduction in the amount of forecast traffic growth would be due to pricing measures.

150 But the failure by Dutch politicians to implement the necessary measures means that Dutch policy is currently failing to meet its long term traffic growth targets. Other policies being tried include, for example, the prioritisation of road space for lorries and high occupancy vehicles.

151 Business people in both Germany and the Netherlands saw future increases in the cost of road transport as inevitable: but they all stressed that such increases should happen on a pan-European basis to lessen the damage to their competitiveness. The move towards greater use of pricing is already taking place with the introduction in 1995 of user charges for HGVs on motorways in Benelux, Denmark and Germany. It should be noted that in the Netherlands and Germany, the introduction of this measure will be offset by a reduction in the level of vehicle excise duty paid by hauliers (placing them at a relative advantage to UK hauliers who will not be given such a rebate).

152 In **France**, pricing has long existed on autoroutes but more as a way of rewarding the concessionaires responsible for autoroute construction/maintenance, rather than as a deliberate policy of demand management. However, consideration is now being given to the use of autoroute tolls explicitly to encourage a shift of HGV traffic from one of the major north-south routes (down the Rhone valley) on to a less congested parallel route.

153 In **the UK**, real term increases in fuel duty in recent and future budgets are presented as deliberate policy to influence driver behaviour and so to help achieve environmental aims. The DoT has also shown interest in the scope for urban road pricing to manage demand by conducting a 3-year study in to the subject, though it remains to be seen what emerges in practice. Government proposals for motorway charging, in addition to their potential for raising new revenue for road investment, also offer scope for managing demand; but there remain considerable fears that this would merely divert traffic to other roads less well-suited to handle such traffic.

A streamlined planning process

154 It is difficult to establish what should be the benchmark for the time taken to plan and build any given transport project (Exhibit 28). Yet delays, especially in securing planning consent for transport projects, is generally seen in all four study countries as an important issue which governments need to address.

This section seeks to give only a general comparison of
experience of the planning system in the four study countries.
It does not try to draw conclusions about what might be a
benchmark for the time taken to plan projects.

One problem is that the differences in the planning periods
may be as much a reflection of the inherent difficulties in
promoting certain projects (eg in terms of scale and location)
as any relative weakness in the process itself. Another
difficulty is that the distinction between the political debate on
the need for a project and the time actually taken to plan and
implement a scheme is not always clear.

In the Netherlands, it takes on average 12 years to design
and build major projects, once an element of certainty on the
availability of national funds has been secured.

In Germany, if the time taken in political debate is discounted,
it can take an average of 9 years to plan a rail project and
10 years for federal roads. The time taken to secure political
confirmation of a proposal can add 3 to 4 years to this
process.

In the United Kingdom, the Department of Transport has
estimated that it takes an average of 13.5 years to plan and
build trunk road schemes.

Sources: Rotterdam City Council, ILS, DoT

155 Frequently, however, one of the major problems
involved is the time taken by the political process to
agree the need for projects in the first place:

- In **the Netherlands**, a change in Government has
  brought into power some of the political opposition
  to the Betuwe rail freight line. This has led to the
  formation of an advisory committee to re-investigate
  the need for the project, thereby delaying its
  construction

- In the **UK**, much of the delay in building the high
  speed rail link to the Channel Tunnel has been due
  to vacillation by Government.

156 In **Germany**, there are plans to seek further
improvements in the planning process, following on
from a recent 'Planning Acceleration Act' for projects
in the former East Germany. This had established
firm timetables for completing the various parts of
the planning process.

157 In the **Netherlands**, the SVV-II includes streamlining
proposals, such as the carrying out in parallel of
different parts of the process by which consent is
required.

158 In **the UK**, changes to public inquiries for road schemes
have recently been proposed by the Department of
Transport as part of a drive to reduce the average
time for planning trunk road schemes by three years.
The impact of this initiative, as with that of the
Transport and Works Act for rail schemes, is as yet
untried.

159 By contrast, planning delay in **France** seems less of
an issue, although there are some exceptions, such
as the TGV Provence or some project proposals near
Paris. This may be due to a combination of factors,
such as the lower population density of France, a
willingness to pay generous compensation to affected
property owners or a frequent readiness on the part
of local communities to see the benefits of new
infrastructure rather than to oppose it.

The use of private finance

160 All four study countries have increasingly been
interested in attracting private investment for transport.
However, the enthusiasm with which this has been
pursued and the approaches adopted differ in each
case. Of the four countries, the UK has perhaps been
most progressive in this field.

161 The **French** argue that they have been attracting
private finance into transport for years. The French
approach places much emphasis on the notion that
private finance is a tool to be used by Government,
through concessions to secure broader strategic aims
(Exhibit 29).

162 In addition, the autoroute concessionaires and SNCF
are allowed by the state to raise funds on the
international capital markets to finance investment.
Although such funds would be considered part of
public sector borrowing in the UK, the autoroute
concessionaires boast that the development of the
French motorway network for the last 20 years has
effectively been achieved at no cost to the French
taxpayer (although Government guarantees have had
to be invoked in the past).

163 Completion of the **German** infrastructure plan depends
on private investment becoming available in the future.
Twelve pilot projects are under way to look at the
scope for private funding and enabling legislation has
been introduced to allow private investors to charge
tolls on new infrastructure from 1998. But in the
view of one major German construction firm - also
involved in one of the consortia bidding for the
Channel Tunnel Rail Link - Germany is about six years
behind the UK in this field.

In **the Netherlands**, Government plans envisage a relatively small, though useful, role for private finance in meeting national objectives, involving a handful of schemes, such as a network of tunnels in the Randstad and the Betuwe rail freight line to Rotterdam. An estimated 4-5 billion guilders between 1994-2003 will be raised by private finance 'and other forms of loan facilities'. While Schiphol Airport has access to the world's debt capital markets, as it is owned by the Dutch State (though capitalised by non-guaranteed

---

Exhibit 29 The French approach to private finance in transport: 'controlled competition'.

The development of public-private partnerships to provide transport infrastructure and services is seen as part of a wider policy to encourage a more market-driven approach to transport by stimulating competition within and between modes. Competition, for the French Transport Minister,

'should be accepted because it encourages reassessment, leading to progress and innovation, but only if it is not considered as an objective governing the whole social fabric but rather as an essential means, serving a global vision of society'.

The underlying principle is one of 'controlled competition' where the public sector defines objectives through infrastructure plans, contracts between state and regions, and between the state and transport providers such as SNCF. At the same time, there is flexibility in choice of provider (private, public, or semipublic), financing structure (conventional loans, private capital, public investment) and share of financial risks.

Autoroutes
Over the last 40 years, the autoroute network has been developed and operated by concessionaire companies. These companies provide financing and collect tolls; the state acquires ownership of the autoroutes as they are built.

Currently, concessionaires divide into two broad types: one private company, operating 740 km (out of a total autoroute network of over 8000 km) and six public-private companies. The latter are being grouped together into three regional areas to improve their financial structure (by grouping profitable and non-profitable motorways) and so remove the need for Government financial support.

Concessionaires enter into five-year contracts with the state, specifying the investment needed and changes in tolls to occur over that period. In the past, Government guarantees (covering, for example, borrowing by concessionaires) have been provided: the position now is that the need for clear risk-sharing between private and public sectors excludes general guarantees by the state.

Railways and urban public transport
SNCF is run as a commercial company whose aim is to operate and develop the national rail network, based on principles (set out by Government decree) of public service. Within this context, SNCF is run by an 'independent management', although the Board of Directors includes representatives of the state.

A five-year contract between the state and SNCF sets out objectives for SNCF and the level of state financial support. Regional rail services are the subject of agreements between SNCF and regions: it is intended that the regions should be given greater independence in defining rail services.

In urban areas, 'organising authorities' (individual communes or groups of communes) are responsible for setting objectives for public transport in their areas. They can either assume direct control of operations or delegate operations to private and semiprivate concessionaires. The state also enters into contracts with the organising authorities, setting out the level of financial assistance from the state.

Airports
France has approximately 560 airfields, half of which were created by the state, the other half by local communities, Chambers of Commerce and other bodies.

Aeroports de Paris (ADP) handles 60% of metropolitan passenger traffic and 85% of metropolitan freight traffic: it is a financially independent public company. It assumes all of its operational and investment costs without any subsidy, although the state reimburses ADP for any charges related to air traffic control and safety. The Government also has a say in the appointment of the President and Managing Director of ADP.

State-owned provincial airports are run under concession by Chambers of Commerce or local communities. While the income generated by the concession is supposed to cover investment and operating costs, the state assumes any outstanding debts, together with the assets, at the end of the concession period.

Ports
There are two types of port in France:

■ 6 autonomous ports (eg Marseilles and Le Havre) handling 52% of the external trade of metropolitan France. They are public companies providing commercial and public services: they benefit from land donated by the state, conferring on the ports management but not ownership of this asset. These ports can grant facilities either through concessions or by allowing private investors temporary use of public quayage.

■ 25 ports of national interest. These ports remained under state control even after the decentralisation of Government in the 1980s due to their economic importance or to enable them to continue providing regional services. In most cases, they are operated under concession by Chambers of Commerce, but in some cases the concessionaire can be a private company.

Source: Ministry of Public Works, Transport and Tourism

debt), this funding (as with the French autoroute companies) would also be considered by the UK Treasury as public sector borrowing.

165 Progress has been generally slow in attracting private sector investment. It has not been particularly forthcoming for the Betuwe rail freight line, although it is essential if the project is to go ahead. Current opposition to the introduction of road pricing has deprived possible private sector investors in road infrastructure of a revenue stream. And the Dutch Government, having experimented with the use of shadow tolls for a scheme in Rotterdam, have rejected their more widespread use on the basis that this is a more expensive way of building infrastructure than if Government had borrowed the necessary funds itself.

166 In the **UK**, the DoT is at the forefront of the Government's initiative to secure private funding for capital projects traditionally funded by the public sector. Some £370 million of private finance has already been invested in transport schemes, with a further £760 million committed.

167 Past successes, such as the Queen Elizabeth II Bridge at Dartford, are to be followed up by a number of schemes either wholly or partly funded by the private sector:

- Birmingham Northern Relief Road

- Channel Tunnel Rail Link

- Heathrow Express and rolling stock for the Northern Line on London Underground

- Design, build, finance and operate (DBFO) schemes for trunk road improvements.

168 The relatively stronger momentum in the UK to tap genuinely new sources of finance has been helped by the Private Finance Panel (made up of members from the private and public sectors, and supported by an executive). The Panel has the specific task of removing obstacles to further private investment and of translating general principles, such as risk-sharing between public or private sectors, into real projects. It does not appear to have a counterpart in the three other countries.

169 However, there are concerns about the initiative. If attracting private finance is to serve the more strategic aim of reversing past under-investment in infrastructure, then it is essential that new funds are made additional to, and not a straightforward

replacement for, public funding. The 1994 Budget, by cutting back heavily on the DoT's spending on roads, raises a major question mark as to whether this is the Government's approach. In addition, it will prove harder to attract potential private investors in future unless the Government can provide greater long-term certainty about the direction of transport policy.

Overall assessment

170 Examination of transport-policy making in the UK, France, Germany and the Netherlands reveals that Governments in these countries face similar challenges.

171 There are relative strengths in the way in which the French, Germans and Dutch face these problems. The Governments in these countries believe good transport links are an important part of the conditions needed to support economic growth.

172 There is a consequent willingness on their part to accept responsibility for overseeing the delivery of those links. This is underpinned by mechanisms which enable a broad consensus to be built on the policies needed to move forward and a willingness to plan over the long term.

173 But there are no panaceas. All Governments face difficulties in bringing together economic and environmental objectives; and all are trying to streamline the ways in which transport schemes make their way from the drawing board to reality. Furthermore, UK policy has scored some notable successes, such as encouraging the private sector to provide transport infrastructure and services.

174 However, the situation faced by the UK is that the quality of its infrastructure compares unfavourably with that of France, Germany and the Netherlands, as well as other major EU states. The three countries compared with the UK also have plans to improve their transport networks even further.

175 For UK business, it is important that our infrastructure is best-in-class. To achieve this, we need to combine and sustain policies which both secure more investment and lead to better management of the capacity of our network.

176 At the same time, given the environmental and public spending constraints faced, we need to look at ways in which the public policy process in the UK can be improved. The final section looks at some ways in which the strengths of policy-making on the Continent might build upon current UK practice to bring about such improvements.

Chapter 4

The way forward for UK transport policy - issues to be resolved

Key principles

177 **The UK decision-making process has to be improved in order to allow better choices to be made by providers and users of transport infrastructure and services.** These choices include:

- The trade-offs involved in developing a transport network which both supports wealth creation and is environmentally sustainable

- The extent to which different types of transport demand - for example, passenger and freight - should have priority in using increasingly-congested networks

- How to provide adequate funding and to establish modal priorities for such funding, to support a desirable level of mobility

- The most efficient use (economically and environmentally) of transport through a mix of signals - investment, revenue support, price, telematics, regulation, restraint.

178 **The process through which those choices are made has to be transparent and understood by all those affected.** These criteria are essential if there is to be greater confidence that the right choices have been made. Recent statements by the Secretary of State provide welcome evidence of growing recognition by Government of the need to build a consensus on transport.

179 As an approach, allowing pure market forces to determine which choices should be made is flawed. **Inherent imperfections in the market for transport emphasise the need for some element of Government intervention:**

- The provision of transport infrastructure and services can be relatively inflexible, particularly in the case of the former (viz the lead-times needed to build new infrastructure): this means that there is frequently a mis-match of demand and supply in the market for transport

- There are external costs and benefits associated with transport which cannot easily be accounted for through the price paid by users

- Transport in practice is a political issue, given the importance people attach to access to jobs and amenities, concern about the environment, and the impact on property rights of building infrastructure.

180 The Government already intervenes in transport, for example, through regulation, investment and financial support for loss-making but socially necessary public transport services. **It follows therefore, that there should be a clear and explicit statement of the sort of transport system the Government is committed to delivering.**

The need for greater government commitment to transport policy

181 **For Governments in Germany, France and the Netherlands, good transport links are a critical underpinning to growth and competitiveness. They therefore accept that they have a responsibility for ensuring that those links are identified and in place. The UK Government should do the same.**

182 The UK Government does recognise that it has a similar responsibility, but not as strongly as Governments in the other study countries. The difference is visible not just in greater past levels of transport investment, but also in the fact that, unlike the UK Government, those in other countries are ready to sign up, politically and financially, to long-term commitments to improve their transport networks.

The need to develop a market for transport which more clearly serves strategic aims

183 The thrust of recent Government policy has to date focused on liberalisation and deregulation mode by mode, in order that market forces may to a large extent determine how and by whom transport services should be provided. While this is fully supported in principle, it has occurred in many ways at the expense of overall infrastructure.

184 The approach of other Governments has focused more on harnessing market forces to deliver the strategic aims which have been set for the transport system as a whole. **The emphasis of UK policy should now see Government concentrate on**

- **Identifying clearly and explicitly a consistent set of strategic economic, social and environmental aims which the market for transport shall serve**

- **Developing a coherent mix of policy levers (investment, pricing, regulation, restraint, etc) - together with an explicit vision of how these will serve the objectives above - which together will shape the market for transport within which the private sector as provider of services and infrastructure can confidently play its part**

- **Accepting more readily and positively that it may have a direct role as facilitator and possibly financier of better links between different modes in pursuit of the aims in the first point.**

185 This approach in some senses is close to the emphasis in French transport policy on 'controlled competition'. There are signs that policy in the UK is increasingly beginning to recognise the merits in such an approach:

- The complex structure of the railways brought home to Government that its original plans for 'on-track' competition between operators were not practical. Through the Franchising Director, the Government will set the pattern for the vast majority of services to be run, and then franchise them to operators; similarly, maintenance of the infrastructure is being put out to tender by Railtrack

- The Government has recently decided not to extend deregulation of bus services to London. Instead, the benefits of private sector management are to be harnessed through competitive tendering to operate routes or a network of routes, without the disadvantages of 'on-street' competition which has characterised some of the deregulated areas outside London.

Turning principles into practice
A policy paper on transport and land use

186 **The first step must be for the UK government to set out what is desirable - economically, environmentally and socially - in terms of developing key transport corridors.** That cannot be done effectively unless there is some vision of the economic and social development of the various parts of the UK: hence the need to co-ordinate transport proposals with those for land use.

187 Government transport policy needs to recognise that - as in other countries over the last 40 years - economic growth will bring with it more traffic. The emphasis for business must be on improving access, through key corridors, to markets in a way which respects the environment as far as possible. This may mean that future construction of infrastructure will become more expensive in order to minimise its impact (eg tunnelling through sensitive areas). This may be the price that Government has to pay - on behalf of society - to ensure that the UK has efficient links which support competitive business.

88 In effect, Government already recognises that it has a role in deciding when, for example, a major project is needed. Applications under the Transport and Works Act for permission to build rail projects can - if the Secretary of State decides they are of national significance - have the issue of need debated in both houses of Parliament. This principle should be extended generally to the overall development of strategic transport links.

89 **A review is needed of the UK's overall transport policy which would cover the objectives and status of all individual major transport modes.** It would also take into account the markets within which they operate (whether national or European as in the case for inland modes, or the wider international markets which confront sea and air transport).

90 **The review should take the form of a policy paper - possibly a Green Paper in the first instance - which draws together a national framework for land use, infrastructure and transport services.** This type of approach was advocated by the CBI in its 1992 document 'Shaping the Nation'.

91 Government currently provides planning guidance at a regional level. The setting of priorities at a regional level itself suggests that Government has some view of how the country as a whole should develop. The proposed policy paper would make more transparent the process by which it arrives at this view, and again would help focus Government policy on providing the sort of transport network needed to deliver strategic objectives.

92 **In keeping with practice on the Continent, such a paper should**

■ **Set out a vision lasting at least 20 years into the future**

■ **Include a five-year rolling programme, reviewed annually to determine the progress of policies in meeting objectives**

■ **Include costings of the measures needed over that period, taking into account possible private finance where that is appropriate.**

93 The preparation of such a vision will clearly take time. **It is essential that this review of policy is not used as an excuse to shelve or delay much-needed investment programmes.** The Secretary of State's recent promise that, in trying to stimulate a properly-

informed debate, he would 'not be putting on hold [his] plans for improving the UK's transport network and reducing the impact of pollution' is encouraging. However, business confidence in that promise needs to be restored after the cuts announced in the Budget and reassessment of national road schemes resulting from the SACTRA report.

Cross-departmental ownership of policy

194 In the interests of minimising policy change, it is also essential that the policy paper on transport has explicit cross-departmental ownership in Whitehall. It was encouraging to note the joint press release, issued by the Departments of Transport, Environment and Health, in response to the Royal Commission on Environmental Pollution's recent report. **Consideration should be given to forming a Cabinet sub-committee on transport, bringing together the DoT, DoE, DTI and Treasury.**

The need for broader consensus on transport policy

195 **There must be an opportunity for the policy paper on transport to be debated in public.** Such a mechanism already exists in the form of Green Papers. These should be adopted for the proposed statement of the Government's vision for transport and land use policy as a whole.

196 **The role of Government at a regional level in helping to shape national policy should also be strengthened in order to widen ownership of this policy.** There may be scope for the new Integrated Regional Offices to play a part in this respect. The IROs should formally be required to consult with, for example, regional planning conferences, local authorities, passenger transport executives (some of whom have already developed strategic approaches to local needs) and the local business community in making recommendations to central Government on national transport priorities during preparation of a Green Paper on transport policy.

A transparent investment appraisal methodology to underpin the building of consensus

197 In order further to inspire public confidence in the process by which transport priorities are set, the investment appraisal methodology used must be seen to be transparent and fair. It may already seem this way as far as the Treasury is concerned. For the voting public, it is neither.

198 **A consistent methodology must be used on main transport corridors to evaluate rival schemes, even if they involve different modes. Only in this way can the public have greater confidence that the merits of all options have been fairly assessed against each other.** This does not necessarily mean that, for example, all road improvements in the national road programme will be dropped in favour of alternative options as a result. But the increased transparency offered by such an approach seems a crucial point in a country where a relatively high population density means that there will frequently be opposition to new infrastructure of any sort.

199 For the same reason, the various criteria against which projects are assessed must be clearly set out. The DoT already uses in effect an informal multi-criteria approach for road schemes. A more formal multi-criteria approach should be adopted across all modes; again, the objective is to make more transparent an important aspect of decision-making.

200 The key factors in determining why certain projects are included, or given different priorities, or dropped from the national plans, should be clearly expressed. The criteria used must give substantial weight to the economic feasibility of projects and must be clearly linked to the strategic objectives set by Government.

A coherent use of policy levers to attract the private sector

201 Potential private sector providers of infrastructure and services will want to minimise the risks to their investments. They will seek long term assurances about the market within which they will be operating before they are willing to make long term commitments. The proposed policy paper, setting out the Government's vision on the strategic development of the transport network, should help provide some of those assurances, particularly on the strategic need on where major projects should be built, with the assurances that there is public acceptance of that need. These need to be supplemented by clear statements on the policy instrument needed to realise that vision, including:

■ The way in which Government policy on funding and pricing will be used to encourage a pattern of modal use (including intermodal links) consistent with strategic objectives

■ The level of Government capital and revenue support for transport infrastructure and services, where there are non-user benefits which cannot be captured through the farebox

■ The extent to which the environmental costs of transport will be accounted for and who should pay for them

■ The extent to which pricing measures should be used to give priority to different types of user, for example between passengers and freight, as well as different types of each

■ A recognition that Government has a role in maintaining a fiscal regime that is conducive to investment (eg in shipping, which operates in global markets, even in trade to, from and within the UK)

■ The nature of Government regulation on areas such as rates of return (eg the RPI-linked formulae used for utilities), level of competition from other providers and the ability of providers to offer services in different modes (eg operating co-ordinated bus and rail services).

Delivering the programme

202 Having set the priorities for developing the country's transport network through public consultation and parliamentary ratification, the delivery of - and particularly the consistency of funding for - improvements to the network needs to be strengthened.

203 In some cases, there will be a straightforward commercial incentive for providers to offer services and infrastructure which also fulfil strategic objectives.

204 **In other cases, there will be, for the foreseeable future, a need for Government to provide funding (both capital and revenue finance) to allow strategically-necessary improvements to proceed. To secure these, Government should develop contracts with providers of transport services and infrastructure (eg the Highways Agency, Railtrack, BAA, rail and public transport operators) to develop the transport network. These contracts should**

■ Last into the medium-term (ie longer than five years) and include a commitment by Government to provide funding where necessary, taking into account likely possible sources of private finance. (There are already precedents for this sort of approach in the UK. Through the Franchising Director, the Government will have to enter into medium-term commitments on the level of revenue support for operators of loss-making rail passenger services: the operators also have the option to provide other services for which they identify a demand).

- Be binding on both sides. Therefore, there should be penalty clauses for avoidable failure to meet commitments on both sides. Reduction or withdrawal of Government investment should only be admissible against the background of serious - and specified - levels of under-performance in the economy as a whole.

- Equally, where public funding is provided for schemes, thought should be given to contractual arrangements whereby Government can share in the profits generated by particularly successful schemes.

05 Consideration should also be given to developing similar contractual arrangements between national Government and Government at a regional level (eg joint arrangements between local authorities) to secure improvements to key routes supporting the strategic transport corridors identified in national policy.

06 The growing provision of infrastructure and services by private sector bodies offers a challenge, but not necessarily a threat, to the development of multi-modal transport strategy and improved links between modes. **Consideration should be given to establishing an Intermodal Panel, bringing together public and private sectors, along the lines of the Private Finance Panel. This should seek to identify obstacles and solutions to providing seamless interchanges between infrastructure and services in different modes, for passengers and freight.** It should be seen as a natural progression of the recent and welcome re-organisation of the DoT along multi-modal lines.

Measuring the performance of Government policy

07 **The five-year rolling policy programme should be subjected to annual scrutiny.** The UK Government already reviews environmental policy annually. The extension of this to transport policy could be part of the current annual report by the Department of Transport and would be very much in keeping with the Government notion of performance-related public services, as exemplified by the Citizen's Charter initiative.

08 To support this scrutiny of policy, the use of performance indicators should be extended. These are already used, for example, to measure progress against the objective of reducing road casualties.

209 **Economic indicators of performance - such as the level of accessibility offered by the road network, which the Highways Agency is working on at the moment - should be developed alongside safety and environmental ones. This would fit well with the current Secretary of State's aims to provide an efficient transport which serves the interests of the economy as well as the community as a whole.**

Conclusion

210 The UK's transport infrastructure is in a relatively poor state. For business and the UK's economic well-being as a whole, improvements are vital. Transport policy needs to be seen to play its part alongside other wider policies to promote economic growth, as outlined in the Government's White Paper on competitiveness.

211 For this reason, the process by which future infrastructure improvements might be achieved is an area of major concern for the CBI. Our analysis suggests that there are some serious weaknesses in the way this process currently operates, compared with some of our major competitors. In our view, two developments are essential for this to be reversed.

212 First, the Government must accept that it has the chief role in setting the framework within which those improvements can be delivered. A key concern in this document has been to look at ways in which Government can exercise its responsibilities, without undermining the contribution that competition and the private sector must make.

213 Second, a broader consensus on transport has to be built on what should be the UK's transport prioroties and how they should be achieved. Making the process of decision-making more transparent will be key to securing this.

214 On the one hand, there is a need for a more 'top-down' approach where policies and their delivery more obviously serve strategic aims. On the other hand, this needs to be paralleled by more of a 'bottom-up' approach wherein the different stakeholders in society have - and feel they have - a more active role in determining those strategic aims.

215 The way forward proposed in this report represent some initial thoughts on how improvements to policy making - and thus improvements to the transport network itself - might be achieved. We intend that they should stimulate debate as a prelude to action.

Acknowledgements

ABB Transportation Ltd

Amey Holdings plc

Associated British Ports

Association des Sociétés Françaises d'Autoroutes

Automobile Association

BAA plc

BACMI Ltd

Bayer AG

B I C C plc

Boots the Chemist Ltd

British Chamber of Commerce in Germany

British Consulate-General, Düsseldorf

British Embassy, Bonn

British Embassy, Paris

British Embassy, The Hague

British Petroleum plc

British Railways Board

British Telecom plc

British Telecom Northern Ireland

Bundesministerium für Verkehr

Bundesministerium für Umwelt, Naturschutz und Reaktorsicherheit

Bundesverband der Deutschen Industrie

Bundesverband Spedition und Lagerei

Cave Wood Transport Ltd

Centre d'études sur les réseaux, les transports, l'urbanisme et les constructions publiques (CERTU)

Chamber of Commerce and Industry for Rotterdam and the Lower-Maas

Chambre de Commerce et d'Industrie de Caen

Chamber of Shipping

Christian Salvesen plc

City of Rotterdam

Conseil Economique et Social Régional de Basse-Normandie

Conseil Général du Calvados: Direction des Services Techniques

Conseil Régional de Basse-Normandie

Conseil Régional d'Ile-de-France

Contship Containerlines Ltd

Coopers & Lybrand

Courage Ltd

Délégation a l'Aménagement du Territoire et à l'Action Régionale (DATAR)

Department of Trade and Industry

Department of Transport

Deutsches Industrie- und Handelstag

Deutsches Verkehrsforum

Direction Générale de l'Equipement, Basse-Normandie

Economic Packaging Ltd

European Centre for Infrastructure Studies

Eurotunnel plc

Federation of Civil Engineering Contractors

Federation National des Transporteurs Routiers

Forte plc

Franco-British Chamber of Commerce and Industry

Freight Transport Association Ltd

GKN Walterscheid GmbH

Hampshire County Council

Hillier Parker May & Rowden

Hochtief AG

IBM United Kingdom Ltd

ICI Polyurethanes

Institut d'Aménagement et d'Urbanisme de la Région d'Ile-de-France (IAURIF)

Institut fur Landes- und Stadtentwicklungsforschung des Landes Nordrhein-Westfalen

Insitut fur Raumplanung, University of Dortmund (Professor Wegener)

John Laing Construction Ltd

John Livingston & Sons Ltd

Karstadt AG

Koninklijke Nedlloyd Groep

London Transport

McAlpine Construction Ltd

Milk Marque

Ministère de l'Economie

Ministère de l'Equipement, du Logement et des Transports

Ministerium für Stadtentwicklung und Verkehr Landes Nordrhein-Westfalen

Ministrie van Economische Zaken

Ministrie van Verkeer en Waterstaat

Ministrie van Verkeer en Waterstaat (Directie Zuid-Holland)

Municipality of Rotterdam

National Power plc

National Express Group plc

Nederlandse Spoorwegen

NFC plc

Nissan Europe

Ove Arup Partnership

Powergen plc

Public Affairs & Marketing Ltd

RAC

Railtrack plc

Railway Industry Association of Great Britain

Road Haulage Association Ltd

Royal Mail

Sceta International

Shell UK Ltd

SMMT Ltd

SNCF

Syndicat des Transports Parisiens

Time & Data Systems International Ltd

Transport 2000

Transport Development Group

UK Petroleum Industries Assn

Unilever

University of Westminster

Vauxhall Motors Ltd

Verbond van Nederlandse Ondernemingen

Vroom and Dreesmann

Welsh Development Agency

Wincanton Distribution Services Ltd

WS Atkins Consultants